This

Nature Storybook

belongs to:

To Charlie and Abigail and to finding your own path. CS

For Andy, with love. MH

First published in 2022
by Walker Books Australia Pty Ltd
Locked Bag 22, Newtown
NSW 2042 Australia
www.walkerbooks.com.au

This edition published in 2023.

The moral rights of the author and illustrator have been asserted.

Text © 2022 Claire Saxby
Illustrations © 2022 Max Hamilton

All rights reserved. No part of this publication may be reproduced, stored in a retrieval system, or transmitted in any form or by any means – electronic, mechanical, photocopying, recording or otherwise – without the prior written permission of the publisher.

A catalogue record for this book is available from the National Library of Australia

ISBN: 978 1 760656 27 0

The illustrations for this book were created with watercolour, aquarelle crayons and coloured pencil.

Typeset in Filosofia and Minik
Printed and bound in China

2 4 6 8 10 9 7 5 3

Set around Narawntapu National Park on Tasmanian north coast to the east of Devonport near Bakers Beach. Long beach, creek, bush and forest. It is October, and the nights are still cool.

Tasmanian Devil

Claire Saxby
Max Hamilton

WALKER BOOKS
AND SUBSIDIARIES
LONDON • BOSTON • SYDNEY • AUCKLAND

A whiskered snout appears at the mouth of a wombat burrow, but it is not a wombat. It is a Tasmanian devil in a borrowed den.

Tasmanian devils use already-dug burrows or tree hollows for shelter and safety from predators, including owls and eagles. Nesting dens are deeper and more secure.

Behind her, in the blue-burrow depths,
two imps curl,
big enough to leave behind,
small enough to need her care.

Three devils in a den,
mother, brother, sister.

Young devils are called imps, joeys or pups. Newborn imps are smaller than your little fingernail. More than 20 imps are born, but there is room in a pouch for a maximum of four.

She is hungry and lopes into the night to search for food. She sniffs the air for the scent of prey or carrion.

Adult devils can eat the equivalent of 40 per cent of their bodyweight each night and may travel up to 16 kilometres before returning home to rest.

In their den, the imps stir.
Nose by nose, they emerge
to peek at their world.

They climb a log and sister leaps on brother.

They wrestle, mouths wide, shrieking and growling at each other.

Adult devils will open wide their mouths, screech and growl at each other if they meet at a carcass. They are mostly scavengers – they feed on dead animals they find, but they also hunt.

Thump! Thump! Thump!
The imps vanish,
too small to be brave,
too young to recognise a wallaby.
Two devils in a den,
waiting to be fed.

After four months, devil imps will be left behind while their mother looks for food. They are curious and very playful.

Their mother returns as dark becomes dawn.
The imps fight for the teats in her pouch,
the pouch they are now too big to ride in.

Imps spend their first four months in their mother's pouch, drinking milk from a teat. Once they are too big for the pouch, they will still feed from the teats for a month or two.

Each night the imps venture further.
Rumble, tumble, climb,
chomp and growl.

Two devils near a den learning what to eat.

When devils hunt small mammals, birds, reptiles, amphibians and insects, they'll eat everything, including bones and fur.

One birdsong morning
their mother does not return.

The day passes,
another night too.

Two devils in a den,
big enough to be alone.

Devil parents do not teach their imps to hunt or scavenge. Devils have a great sense of smell and can smell food from up to one kilometre away.

As a third night falls, two heads
appear at the mouth of a den.
Two devils roam the beach,
wrestling,
shrieking,
scavenging.

Devils will eat dead fish
and other sea creatures
from the tideline.
Relative to its size, an adult
devil has a bite stronger
than that of a tiger.

He skims the tidal creek.

She lopes the darkling scrub.

Once they are independent, devils live a mostly solitary life. Sometimes they will gather at a carcass, when that carcass is more than enough for one. Sharing a carcass always involves screeching and fighting.

Two devils on their own,
big enough to find their
own dens.

Hungry.

Information about Tasmanian devils

Tasmanian devils got their name from the howls and screeches they make in the night. They are only found in Australia's island state, Tasmania, although they once also roamed the mainland too. Devils are nocturnal and quite shy. They live in a variety of habitats from the mountains to the sea and have also adapted to live near farmland. The Tasmanian devil is the world's largest carnivorous marsupial with a powerful jaw that opens to 70 to 80 degrees.

Adults can weigh 10 to 12 kilograms and stand about 30 centimetres at the shoulder. Their front legs are longer than their back legs and they are good climbers and swimmers. Individual markings can vary, although most have some form of white stripe on their chest. Devil facial tumour disease has reduced their numbers to the point they are now considered endangered in the wild.

Index

Look up the pages to find out about all these Tasmanian devil things.

Don't forget to look at both kinds of words – this kind and this kind.

About the author

Claire Saxby lives in Melbourne, Australia and loves her city. She is the bestselling and award-winning author of many books. *There Was an Old Sailor* (illustrated by Cassandra Allen) won the Society of Children's Book Writers and Illustrators Crystal Kite Award. *Big Red Kangaroo* and *Emu* (both illustrated by Graham Byrne) and *Koala* (illustrated by Julie Vivas) have won numerous awards. *Dingo* (illustrated by Tannya Harricks) was joint winner of the Patricia Wrightson Prize for Children's Literature at the NSW Premier's Literary Award (2019) and *Kookaburra* (illustrated by Tannya Harricks) was a Children's Book Council of Australia Notable book (2021).

About the illustrator

Max Hamilton is an award-winning illustrator, graphic designer and, most enthusiastically, a maker of children's books. She enjoys noticing the little details in things, loves to get lost in the world of illustration and stories and, through her art, aims to raise awareness of the importance of protecting our Australian fauna.

Max lives in Sydney with her partner, two daughters, a fluffy dog and two guinea pigs named Dumpling and Noodles.

Nature Storybooks

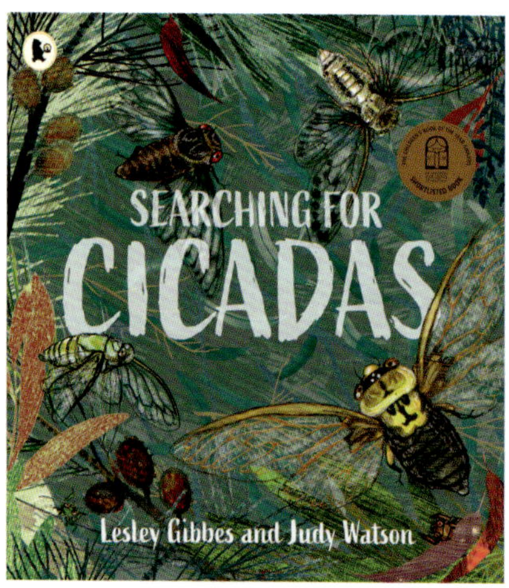

SEARCHING FOR CICADAS
by Lesley Gibbes
illustrated by Judy Watson

WINNER, CHILDREN'S STORY, WHITLEY AWARDS

SHORTLISTED, EVE POWNALL AWARD, CBCA BOOK OF THE YEAR AWARDS

"Evocative illustrations perfectly depict the Australian bush. A fun way to learn about cicadas."

The Sunday Telegraph

". . . stunning. Readers will pore over the pages looking at the incredible detail included on each page . . . Highly recommended."

ReadPlus

Paperback 978-1-760655-48-8

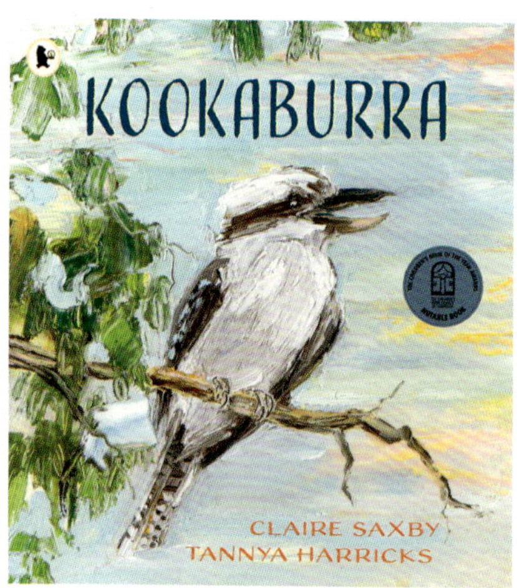

KOOKABURRA
by Claire Saxby
illustrated by Tannya Harricks

NOTABLE, EVE POWNALL AWARD, CBCA BOOK OF THE YEAR AWARDS

"This book is exceptional. It is an absolute must for school and public libraries and would make the perfect gift for all ages."

Magpies

"This is a superb title to share with children at home or as a non-fiction narrative in the classroom . . . the perfect choice for budding wildlife experts."

CBCA: *Reading Time*

"Nature Storybooks open countless opportunities to younger readers, to identify and learn about Australian animals and birds . . . Gorgeous."

Kids' Book Review

Paperback 978-1-760655-02-0

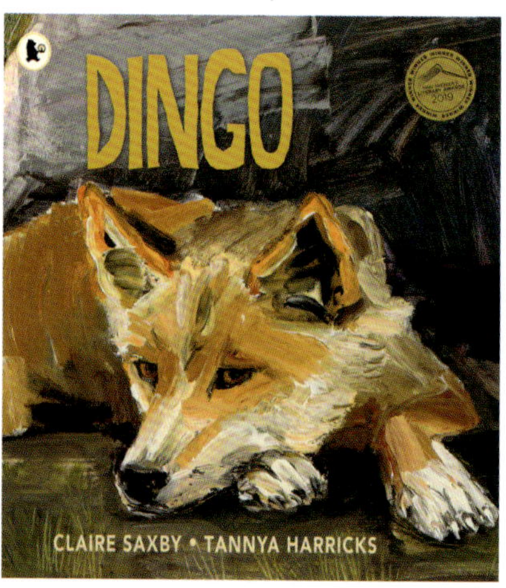

DINGO
by Claire Saxby
illustrated by Tannya Harricks

WINNER, PATRICIA WRIGHTSON PRIZE FOR CHILDREN'S LITERATURE, NSW PREMIER'S LITERARY AWARDS

SHORTLISTED, AWARD FOR NEW ILLUSTRATOR, CBCA BOOK OF THE YEAR AWARDS

"A tawny antipodean hunter pads through Tannya Harricks's gorgeous, impressionistic oil paintings . . . a double-text approach allows the book to be read at two levels, with the larger writing following a particular female dingo as she hunts, while the smaller writing conveys facts about the nature and habits of these wild dogs. With thick brushstrokes, Ms. Harricks summons the sered land and low trees of the Australian bush, the unseen moon turning the ground almost white as the dingo hunts for a rabbit to feed her pups. It's a beautiful tribute to an often-maligned animal, and wonderful to read aloud."

The Wall Street Journal

Paperback 978-1-760651-56-5